Rabbits, Rabbits

Rabbits, Rabbits

Poems by
AILEEN FISHER

illustrated by
Gail Niemann

HARPER & ROW, PUBLISHERS

Designed by Ellen Weiss
1 2 3 4 5 6 7 8 9 10
First Edition

Library of Congress Cataloging in Publication Data
Fisher, Aileen Lucia, 1906–
Rabbits, rabbits.

"A Charlotte Zolotow book."
Summary: Presents twenty-one illustrated poems about rabbits.
1. Rabbits—Juvenile literature. 2. Children's poetry, American. [1. Rabbits—Poetry. 2. American poetry] I. Niemann, Gail, ill. II. Title.
PS3511.I7294R3 1983   811'.52   82-48849
ISBN 0-06-021896-7
ISBN 0-06-021899-1 (lib. bdg.)

Other Books by Aileen Fisher

Anybody Home?
Easter
Going Barefoot
I Stood Upon a Mountain
Like Nothing at All
Listen, Rabbit
Once We Went on a Picnic
Out in the Dark and Daylight
Sing, Little Mouse

Early Spring

Rabbit,
with those ears you grow
you should be
the first to know
signs of Spring
before they *show*:

Trees telling
of buds swelling,

Earth rousing
from long drowsing,

Hills shouting
of grass sprouting...

Hearing things
before they show,
with those great big
ears you grow,
you should be
the first to know,
Rabbit.

Secrets

The morning the first Spring bluebird
said "Hi!" to the thawing tree,
nobody heard but the Rabbit,
the Cottontail Rabbit,
and me.

The morning the Easter daisy
opened its eye to see,
nobody knew but the Rabbit,
the Cottontail Rabbit,
and me.

The morning the new grass started
to put on its greenery,
nobody saw but the Rabbit,
the Cottontail Rabbit,
and me.

We don't look alike or act it,
but secretly we agree,
so I wink an eye at the Rabbit,
and he flicks a whisker
at me.

Spring Fever

When green tints the meadow
and gold shines the tree
and Winter is over
and rivers run free,
do you feel all leapy
and hoppy... like *me*,
Rabbit?

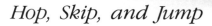

Hop, Skip, and Jump

Rabbits have habits
I wish could be mine:
running and jumping like that
would be fine,
leaping and hopping
so far and so fast
would make me the winner
...instead of the *last.*

But Rabbits

Bullfrogs sing
in the bogs in Spring,

Peepers peep
when the dark is deep,

Birds are gay
on a bright green day,

But Rabbits rejoice
without a voice:

They leap and dance
on a night in Spring
but never, oh, never,
are heard to sing.

Rabbit World

Rabbits live in a meadow world
with carpets wall to wall
and rabbity picnics spread about…
four-leaf clovers and all.

Clover Rain

Ho, you Rabbits,
gray-and-brown,
don't be wearing
such a frown;
not just clouds
are falling down...
all that rain
from April's cup
starts grass and clover
springing up!

Run, Rabbit!

You're not a very good fighter,
Rabbit.
Your claws aren't much better
than none.
You can't match a dog as a biter,
Rabbit,
but oh, how you're able to run!

Bulgy Eyes

A Rabbit's eyes are bulgy-out
and placed so they can look about
frontward, sideward, left and right
at everything that comes in sight.

So, sitting in his grassy bed,
a Rabbit needn't turn his head
to see what's going on about...
with eyes so big and bulgy-out.

Who Scans the Meadow?

Who scans the meadow up and down
from where his little niche is?

Who wears a coat of grayish brown
with grayish-brownish britches?

Who hurries, full of leaps and hops,
across the fields and ditches?

Whose mouth is full of clover tops,
whose nose is full of twitches?

Easter Morning

We went out on an Easter morning
under the trees and the blue-silk sky,
up to the hill where the buds were swelling...
Mother, Father, and Puck and I.

And I had hopes that we'd see a Rabbit,
a brown little one with a cotton tail,
so we looked in the woods and under the bushes
and followed what seemed like a rabbit trail.

We peeked and poked. But there wasn't a Rabbit
wherever we'd look, wherever we'd go.
And then I remembered, and said, *"No wonder.*
Easter's their busiest day, you know!"

Color Blind

Poor little Rabbits...
although your noses
smell very well, and your ears are keen,
you can't see the color
of grass or roses,
can't see yellow or red or green.

Poor little Rabbits...
never once knowing
color of poppies or bluebird blue—
black and white only,
or grayish, showing
in sky, and meadow, and woods for you.

To a Lady Cottontail

Your life is simple, Rabbit.
Your rabbit wants are small:
you only need a place to crouch
and not a house at all...

Until it's time for babies,
and then you're all astir—
you line a little hollow
with silky grass and fur,
and even make a blanket
of rabbit fur and grass
to keep your babies warm and safe,
should anybody pass.

Ready...Set...

Rabbit, crouch for safety
where the shadows cling,

Crouch for warmth and cover
with branches sheltering,

But always keep your hinges
ready...set...to spring!

Cotton Tails

When Cottontails scrunch
under spruces and willows
and munch little clovers
and daffy-down-dillows,
their tails make them soft
little cottony pillows.

Jack Rabbit

Jack Rabbit sits
in a shallow hollow
next to a weed
or a bush or tree;
Summer may come
and Winter follow—
there in the open
Jack will be.

Near at hand
live the ones roofed over:
mole in his tunnel,
mouse in her nest,
but Jack Rabbit sits
in the snow or clover,
liking his roof
of sky the best.

Says the Rabbit

"I don't ask for much,"
says the Rabbit.
"I'm peaceful and quiet all day.
I don't ask for more
than a brush pile
and clover to nibble, or hay,
and a small piece of pasture
to run in...
and dogs that will *please stay away.*"

Beneath the Snowy Trees

When boughs of spruces bend with snow
to way below their knees,
little caves and caverns show
beneath the snowy trees...
caves so secret, caves so low,
I think it would be fun
to be a Rabbit who could go
and look in every one.

Snowshoe Hare

We clomp through the snow
from here to there,
but that isn't so
with a Snowshoe Hare:
his long hind feet
make a very good pair
of snowshoes, fit
for a Hare to wear.

Whisk! He covers
the snow with ease,
dashing along
as fast as you please,
while we go plodding
among the trees,
making footprints
that reach *our knees.*

Do Rabbits Have Christmas?

Do Rabbits have Christmas,
I wonder, I wonder?

They have little spruces
to celebrate under,
where snow has made pompons
with silvery handles,
and frost has made tinsel
and icicle candles.

Do Rabbits have presents,
I wonder, I wonder?

They have little fir trees
to celebrate under.
But do they have secrets
and smiles on their faces?
Let's go put some carrots
in rabbity places!

Thinking

Wouldn't it be funny
if, somehow, we could shrink
and turn into a Bunny
and learn what Bunnies think?